THE LOVED HAUNTS

OF

COWPER,

BEING AN OUTLINE OF THE LIFE OF WILLIAM COWPER
WITH SPECIAL REFERENCE TO HIS FAVOURITE
RESORTS IN OLNEY AND
WESTON UNDERWOOD

TO WHICH IS APPENDED A

POEM BY JOHN NEWTON,

ENTITLED

"The Supposed Meeting of Cowper and Newton in Heaven."

BY

THOMAS WRIGHT,

Author of "The Life of William Cowper," "The Town of Cowper,"
"The Life of Daniel Defoe," "The Mystery of St. Dunstan's." &c.

LONDON: T. FISHER UNWIN.

1894.

COWPER BY JACKSON.

This book was given

to the library

in memory

of

Charles Frederic Hardy

Author of

"The Hardys of Barbon," etc.

by his wife

1929

ILLUSTRATIONS.

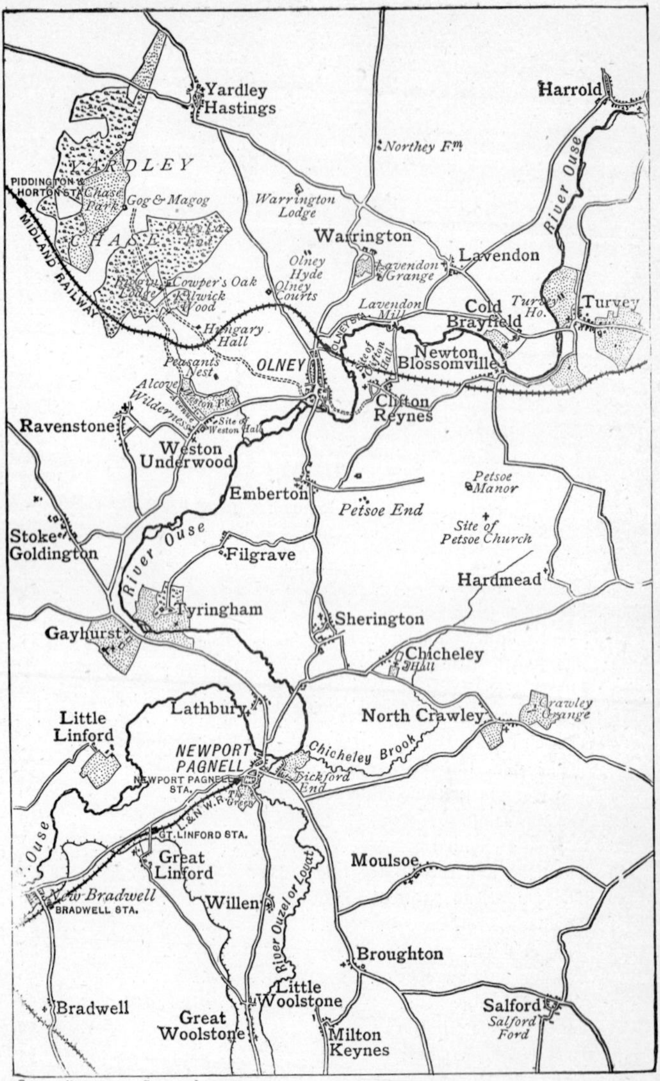

MAP OF OLNEY AND ENVIRONS.

COWPER MEMORIAL CHURCH, OLNEY.

The Loved Haunts of Cowper.

I.

GREAT BERKHAMSTED AND WESTMINSTER.

William Cowper, the celebrated poet and charming letter-writer, was born at the Rectory House of Great Berkhamsted, on Nov. 26, 1731, his father being the Rev. John Cowper, D.D., rector of the parish, and his mother, Anne, daughter of Roger Donne, Esq., of Ludham Hall, Norfolk.

At the old "Pastoral House," as he lovingly calls it, William Cowper spent the happy days of his early childhood, becoming attached to every tree, gate, and stile in the neighbourhood, preferring his own house to a palace, and supposing as a matter of course that he and his father and mother were going to live in it always. Cowper ever retained a very vivid recollection of these early days at Berkhamsted.

On November 7, 1737, was born Cowper's brother John, the only child of Dr. Cowper, beside William, that grew to manhood; a few days later, on the 13th, the mother died, at the early age of 34. William, was only "six years old," yet such an impression had her affection and tenderness made on his mind that fifty years afterwards, on receiving her picture, he "dwelt as fondly on the cherished features as if he had just mourned her death." Writing to his cousin, Mrs. Bodham, who had sent him the portrait, he says, "I received it the night before last, and viewed it with a trepidation of nerves and spirits somewhat akin to what I should have felt had the dear original presented herself to my embraces. I kissed it, and hung it where it is the last object that I see at night, and of course the first on which I open my eyes in the morning."

THE PARSONAGE, GREAT BERKHAMSTED.

COWPER'S MOTHER.

His lines, "On the Receipt of my Mother's Picture out of Norfolk," form one of the most touching elegies in the language. How pathetic, for example, is the following :—

"My mother! when I learned that thou wast dead,
Say, wast thou conscious of the tears I shed?
Hovered thy spirit o'er thy sorrowing son,
Wretch even then, life's journey just begun?
Perhaps thou gavest me, though unfelt, a kiss;
Perhaps a tear, if souls can weep in bliss—

> Ah, that maternal smile!—it answers—Yes.
> I heard the bell tolled on thy burial day,
> I saw the hearse that bore thee slow away,
> And, turning from my nursery window, drew
> A long, long sigh, and wept a last adieu!"

To his friend Hill, after the lapse of forty-seven years, he wrote: "I can truly say, that not a week passes (perhaps I might with equal veracity say a day) in which I do not think of her: such was the impression her tenderness made upon me, though the opportunity she had for showing it was so short."

Mrs. Cowper was buried at Berkhamsted. Soon after his mother's death, William, at the age of six, was sent to a large boarding school, where he experienced much cruel treatment from older and rougher boys; and the two years spent there were remarkable only for their wretchedness.

He was removed on account of serious inflammation in his eyes, and placed under the care of Mr. Disney, an eminent oculist; and at the age of ten, when sufficiently recovered, was entered at Westminster, where he was the schoolfellow of Warren Hastings, Elijah Impey, Robert Lloyd, Charles Churchill, Richard Cumberland, George Colman the elder, and Bonnell Thornton, all of whom rose to distinction and fame.

II.

SOUTHAMPTON ROW AND THE TEMPLE.

He left school when about eighteen, and after spending nine months at Berkhamsted, was sent to acquire the practice of the law with Mr. Chapman, an attorney. But his time was spent not so much at Mr. Chapman's as in Southampton Row, with his cousins Harriet (afterwards Lady Hesketh) and Theodora, where, as he himself tells us, he and his fellow-student, Thurlow, the future Lord Chancellor, were "constantly employed from morning to night in giggling and making giggle, instead of studying the law." In 1752 he took chambers in the Temple, and here it was that he first experienced that melancholy and depression of spirits which afterwards assumed so serious a form.

Among his acquaintances at the Temple were Carr, Allston, and Clotworthy Rowley; and it may have been to one of these, that he wrote the two earliest preserved letters of his, which begin "Dear Toby."

The first, dated Feb. 21, 1754, contains an allusion to his cousin Theodora, with whom he had now fallen in love. In the postscript he says—You may remember that there was some small difference between me and the person I hinted at in the beginning of my letter; the enclosed was written upon that subject since I saw you last. All is comfortable and happy between us at present, and I doubt not will continue so for ever. Indeed we had neither of us any great reason to be dissatisfied, and perhaps quarrelled merely for the sake of the reconciliation, which you may be sure made ample amends. Adieu!

The second letter, which is undated, is a very curious one.

"Great Berkhamsted, I don't know when.

Dear Toby—I am in such a hurry, I hardly know how to set one leg before t'other to get to the end of my letter, and God knows if I shall be able to do it to night. Dancing all last night, in bed one half of the day, and shooting all the other half, and am now going to—what? to kill a boding screech owl perched upon a tree just by my window. Have at you old Wise Acre. What an Irishman am I? I went to destroy one of Dame Dallas' poultry, and she to defend her songster cast a cloud before my eyes, and behold, I could not see to the end of my gun. I have had no time, Toby, to versify for you except what I stole under a hedge to-day, while I was shooting, so there I sat me down with my pencil in my hand and my gun by my side, in *utrumque paratus*."

This is followed by "a piece of a rare song" which he had recently heard, and some verses in Latin of his own composition.*

Unfortunately, Mr. Ashley Cowper, Theodora's father, refused his consent to Cowper's union with his daughter.

This decision was accepted on both sides as final, Cowper took his farewell of her about 1756, and they never afterwards

* These letters have never before been printed except in *The Archivist* for June, 1892, where they are given in full.

met. After many years had passed by, when in the height of his fame, he received at different times several handsome presents from an anonymous donor, who, though he himself never suspected it, was doubtless his cousin Theodora. Now it was a writing desk, the same that figures in his portrait by Abbot, now an elegant snuff-box, with a representation of the Peasant's Nest on the lid. Sometimes even sums of money came just as anonymously. Theodora Cowper died unmarried in 1825.

About two years after parting from her, Cowper fell in love with another young lady, "a lovely and beloved little girl of sixteen," who lived at Greenwich, but, whose name is not given us; before long, however, she departed to her birthplace in the West Indies, and Cowper was a second time left disconsolate.

In 1756, shortly after the death of his father, Cowper bade his last adieu to Berkhamsted, its fields and woods, and the old parsonage that was so familiar to him. Whilst at the Temple he was a member of the Nonsense Club, a society of literary triflers, Westminster men all of them, who dined together every Thursday: and he contributed a few papers to "The Connoisseur," and "produced several halfpenny ballads, two or three of which had the honour to become popular." He was now presented by his kinsman, Major Cowper, to the office of Clerk of the Journals to the House of Lords, a desirable and lucrative appointment, but doubly welcome to Cowper, for his patrimony was small, and fear of poverty was making his life miserable. But no sooner had he accepted it than he found he would be obliged to qualify himself at the bar of the House; and such was his sensitiveness, that the dread of the examination threw him into the deepest distress and misery. Having brooded over his accumulated troubles till worked up to a fit of madness, he attempted to commit suicide; and, thereupon, was removed to a private asylum at St. Albans kept by Dr. Cotton, where, although his health and reason were regained in about four months, he stayed altogether a year and a half.

III.

ST. ALBANS AND HUNTINGDON.

In the realistic and touching "Song of Mercy and Judgment," written about this time, and first published in 1891, Cowper celebrates his recovery with intense thankfulness and joy.

His income, through the kindness of his relations, having been made enough to keep him, Cowper determined not to return to London, but to retire to some quiet place in the country; and, so as to be near his brother John, who resided at Cambridge, decided on Huntingdon. It was about the time this change was made that he wrote the hymns, "How blest Thy creature is, O God," and "Far from the world, O Lord, I flee."

Among the actions of Cowper just before leaving St. Albans were two that were very characteristic of him. In the first place he persuaded Dr. Cotton to surrender to him his servant Sam Roberts, and in the second he took upon himself the charge of a necessitous boy, named Richard Coleman—notwithstanding, too, the knowledge that in consequence of the lowness of his income he would himself for the future be obliged to depend upon the bounty of friends.

In reference to Roberts, Cowper says, "He had maintained such an affectionate watchfulness over me during my whole illness, and waited on me with so much patience and gentleness, that I could not bear to leave him behind, though it was with some difficulty that the doctor was prevailed on to part with him."

As regards the boy, that Cowper's motive was good, no one wishes to deny, but unfortunately, it was a piece of generosity at the expense of other people. And if keeping a necessitous boy was being generous with other people's money, what was keeping a man-servant that he could certainly have done without? The expense of maintaining Dick Coleman, whom he subsequently apprenticed to a breeches-maker, was for some years a constant source of anxiety to Cowper. But this was not the worst, for the boy turned out badly, and grew up to be idle, intemperate and generally worthless.

At Huntingdon, Cowper formed an intimacy, and took up his abode with the Unwins, the amiable family with whose virtues and graces his letters have made us so familiar. The father, the Rev. Morley Unwin, was "a Parson Adams in simplicity," the daughter, a young lady of eighteen, "handsome and genteel;" but to us the more interesting members of this

MRS. UNWIN.

little circle are the mother, Mary Unwin, "of a very uncommon understanding, who had read much to excellent purpose, and was more polite than a duchess;" and the son, William

Cawthorne, known to posterity as the beloved friend and one of the most favoured correspondents of the poet. In June 1767, Mr. Unwin met with his death from an accident, and thereupon Mrs. Unwin and Cowper, towards whom "her behaviour had always been that of a mother to her son," resolved to leave Huntingdon, desiring to remove to some town or village where they would be under an evangelical minister of the Gospel. Whilst undecided whither to go, a visitor arrived, the Rev. John Newton of Olney, who had been requested to call on them by Dr. Conyers, a Cambridge friend of young Unwin, and it was soon arranged that they should come and reside at Olney. The removal took place on Sept. 14, 1767.

IV.

OLNEY.

The town of Olney, in which Cowper had now settled, and which, owing to his connection with it, was to get to itself so much fame, consisted, and still consists, of one long, broad street, widening southward into a spacious triangular market-place, on the south side of which stands the large red-bricked house with stone dressings, sometimes called Orchard Side, which was to be for nineteen years the poet's home. The most conspicuous object in the town is the church with its tall steeple, and the most noticeable feature of the surrounding country is the River Ouse, that winds tortuously through the level meadows. The villages of Emberton, Weston Underwood, Clifton, and Lavendon lie respectively south, west, east, and north, at a distance of a mile and a mile and a half; all of them more or less associated with the poet's name. The small town of Newport Pagnell is five miles due south.

Thanks to several old sketches we are able to get a pretty accurate idea of the appearance of Olney in the days of Cowper. One view, taken, at the beginning of the century, from the end of Weston Road, shows the old-fashioned shops and bow-windows, the "Bull" with its sign-board and gilded grapes, then the "Saracen's Head" with its sign-post out in the road, and next, the narrow lane intervening, the shop of William Wilson, the poet's barber, showing bravely its parti-

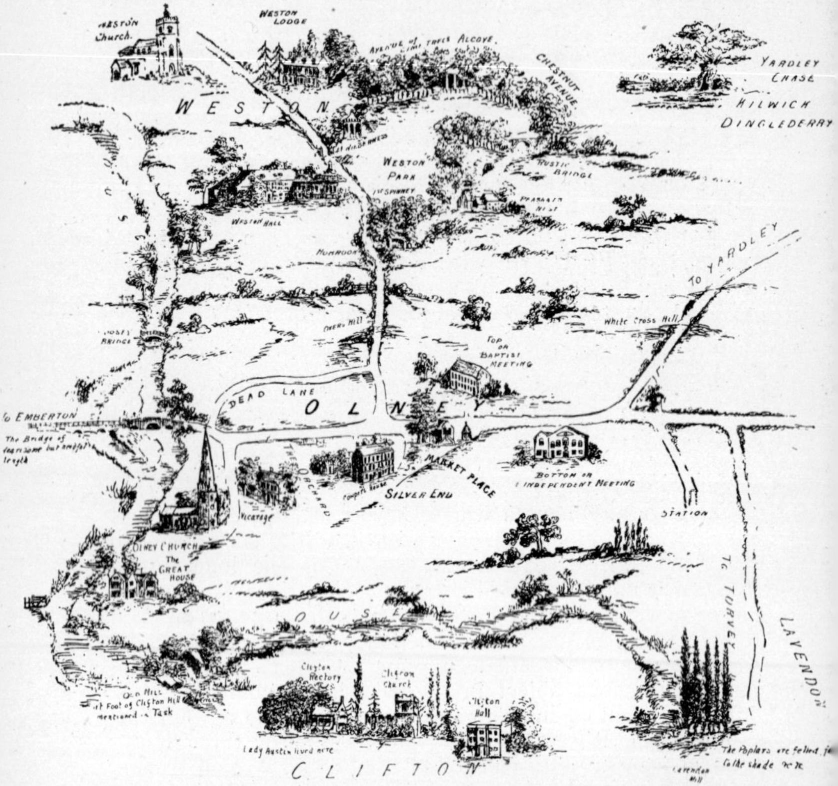

BIRD'S EYE VIEW OF OLNEY AND WESTON UNDERWOOD.

Clifton Hall and the Independent Meeting have been purposely made to face east. In reality they faced west.

coloured pole. On the other side of the way we notice the "Swan," "where they are excessively careless," and where letters are sometimes overlooked, and do not reach their destination, if no enquiry be made, till some days have passed after their arrival in Olney. This was the inn to which the immortal postboy ("Task," iv.) used to consign his "important budget:"—

OLNEY CHURCH. *(From photograph.)*

"He comes, the herald of a noisy world,
With spattered boots, strapped waist, and frozen locks,
News from all nations lumbering on his back.
True to his charge, the close-packed load behind,
Yet careless what he brings, his one concern
Is to conduct it to the destined inn,
And having dropped the expected bag—pass on."

In the middle of the market place stood three fine elms, which overshadowed a curious old two-storied stone building called the Shiel Hall. At the end facing north was a double flight of steps leading to the upper room, which answered for Olney the purpose of a Town Hall, and on each side the doorway of this room was a large bow-window. At its south end stood several cottages and a blacksmith's forge. To the north-east of the Shiel Hall was another conspicuous object, the Round House, Stone House or town prison, a small hexagonal building; from which to the High Arch (the rise in the road near the Independent Meeting) and back again

THE CHURCHYARD ELM.

was the ancient whipping-distance for Olney. Down the middle of the main street of the town ran a pitched causeway, with posts at regular distances. It commenced near the Swan Inn (in the market-place), and ended near "The Churchyard Elm," an ancient hollow tree, still standing, that m arked the boundary of the old churchyard of Olney. Along the west side of the High Street from Spring Lane to the High Arch ran a stream of clear water lined by willow trees, which was met by another stream which proceeded from the Yardley Road. The combined waters poured through the High Arch, and flowed thence into the river. The Shiel Hall was taken down about 1816, the Round House about 1846. Of the three elms referred to, one seems to have disappeared before the commencement of the present century, another was blown down about 1832, and the third was partially destroyed in July, 1884. For the rest, the houses were most of them thatched, and as in the old coaching days there was a deal of traffic through the town, publichouses were particularly numerous.

"The bridge of wearisome but needful length" bestrode the valley between Olney and Emberton. Its appearance was most singular. The arches were at irregular distances, and of various sizes. Some had distinctive names; that, for instance, nearest the old bridge being called the Constable Arch. The causeway, was lined on both sides by wooden railings, in which in several places openings were left, so that by means of stone steps one could descend into the meadows. It was taken down in 1832, when its successor, a very much shorter bridge, was erected. The ancient bridge over the mill stream is, at the moment of writing, being demolished, a new structure of iron being destined to take its place.

At the time Cowper and Mrs. Unwin reached Olney, the vicarage was being enlarged and almost rebuilt by Lord Dartmouth, and it was not finished until October 23rd, on which day, Newton removed thither, his new friends accompanying him.

Instead of "one of the most inconvenient," Newton now found the vicarage "one of the best and most commodious houses in the county." Cowper described it as "a smart, stone building, well sashed, much too good for the living." At the present day, mellowed by time, the newly-built, "well-sashed" house of Cowper's letters, is just beginning to look

T. SULMAN
EER

venerable.

On the 9th of Dec., Cowper and Mrs. Unwin removed to Orchard Side.

In his poetical epistle to Lady Austen, Cowper describes his house as

"Deep in the abyss of Silver End."

Nothing, however, but poetical licence justifies him in so describing it. It was not the most agreeably situated house in the town truly, for to live even on the verge of what might be called the Alsatia of Olney must have been accompanied with certain disadvantages; but it faces the market-hill, its situation is far from unpleasant, and on the whole, Cowper made himself very comfortable in it.

COWPER'S HOUSE, OLNEY. *(From a photograph.)*

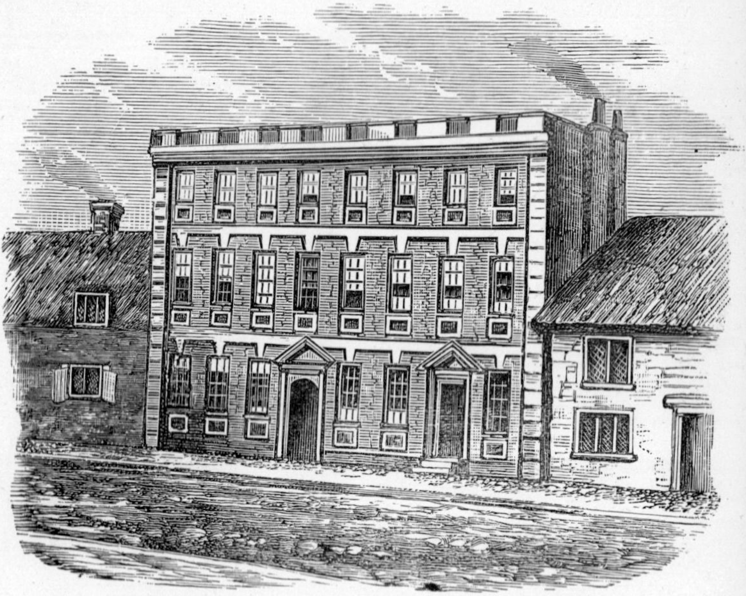

COWPER'S HOUSE IN THE TIME OF COWPER.

(The windows of the world-famous parlour, are those between the two doors.)

In the poet's time Orchard Side had a cornice and imitation embattlements which hid the roof, and two doors instead of three.

To its castellated appearance Cowper himself refers in a letter to Unwin (July 3, 1786), written just after his removal to Weston. At first sight of the odd-looking place Unwin was shocked. In his eyes it had the appearance of a prison, and he did not like the thought of his mother living in it. Says Cowper: "Your view of it was not only just, but prophetic. It had not only the aspect of a place built for the purposes of incarceration, but has actually served that purpose through a long, long period, and we have been the prisoners. But a gaol-delivery is at hand; the bolts and bars are to be loosed, and we shall escape."

The part of the house occupied by Cowper and Mrs. Unwin —for they never occupied the whole—was the western half, which is the farther of the two from Silver End. It should be borne in mind in reading this description that Cowper's House faces north.

THE SUMMER-HOUSE.

The yard at the back of the house, which reminds of the incident of the viper, celebrated in the poem called "The Colubriad," was followed by a long narrow garden threaded by a gravel path thirty yards long, at the end of which stood the small erection called "The Summer House," which for the greatness of its renown rivals even Cowper's world-famous parlour. This tiny building, "not much bigger than a sedan chair," which Cowper sometimes called his boudoir, had formerly served an apothecary as a smoking-room; and in the floor is still the trap door, "which," says Cowper, "covered a hole in the ground where he (the apothecary) kept his bottles;" the same hole in which Mr. Bull, who visited Olney once a fortnight, used to keep his pipes and tobacco.

Between the poet's garden and the vicarage garden was an orchard—Mrs. Aspray's orchard—the same that gave the name to Cowper's house; and in order that Cowper and his friend Newton might be able to visit each other without going through the street, they had a doorway made through the vicarage garden wall. For the privilege of passing through the orchard they paid a guinea a year, and hence the name by which it is generally known—Guinea Field.

As regards the interior of Cowper's House, the passage into which the front door now opens, and the small room on the right as you enter the house, were formerly one, and formed Cowper's hall. With this exception, the inside of the portion occupied by the poet is much the same as it was in his own day. The small casement at the back of the hall through which "Cowper's hares used to come leaping out to their evening gambols on the carpet," is now plastered up, but it can still be seen from the kitchen behind.

The parlour of world-wide fame, a square room, has two windows (still retaining their shutters) in front, and had formerly, besides the door opening into the hall, two other doors exactly opposite the windows, one opening on to a staircase, the other (now removed) belonging to a cupboard. The chimney is wainscoted, as are the walls for about a yard from the ground. As regards size, the parlour is now the same as it was in Cowper's time, but the door between the parlour and the hall was a couple of yards farther from the street than the present one.

The poet's favourite seat in the daytime was at the second window from the front door; but perhaps we like best to think of him in that front room on a winter's evening, and to picture him giving expression to his well-known lines in the Fourth Book of "The Task:"—

"Now stir the fire, and close the shutters fast,
Let fall the curtains, wheel the sofa round,
And while the bubbling and loud-hissing urn

Throws up a steamy column, and the cups
That cheer but not inebriate, wait on each,
So let us welcome peaceful evening in."

These first three months were spent very happily. So far from being a recluse, Cowper, in company with Newton, visited all the country round, and the intercourse between the friends, became very close and affectionate. "For six years," says Newton, "we were seldom separate, when at home and awake." Much of their time was spent in visiting the poor, ministering to the sick, and praying at the bedside of the dying. In the midst of these labours Cowper lost his only brother John, to whose character and worth he alludes in "The Task," II.

HIGH STREET SOUTH, OLNEY.

In 1771, struck with the increasing gloom that was enveloping his friend, Newton suggested the writing of the Olney Hymns, in the hope that concentration of mind on holy themes would afford relief; but ere the former had completed his share the old and dreaded malady again seized him, and he was deranged for a third time (January 1773.) A month later, he had an awful Dream in which "a word was spoken," and this dream had such an effect on him, that ever after, he believed himself to be damned.*

The first of the hymns by Cowper, is the beautiful "Oh for a closer walk with God!"; "Hark, my soul! it is the Lord," and "Jesus, where'er Thy people meet," are gems both of them; and the hymn commencing, "Sometimes a light surprises," is scarcely less precious. "Jesus, where'er Thy people meet," was composed for the use of the worshippers at the "Great House," an old mansion near the church where prayer meetings were held; the hymns entitled "Submission," and "Welcome Cross," were probably suggested by the loss of his brother John. The last written by Cowper, and perhaps the finest of all, is "God moves in a mysterious way," said to have been composed after the frustration of a plan to destroy himself.

In consequence of his derangement the engagement of marriage which had been contracted between Cowper and Mrs. Unwin two or three years previous was broken off. They were to have been married in a few months. Mrs. Unwin was now forty-eight years of age, Cowper forty-one.

At first Cowper refused all medicines, but in accordance with the wish of his Aunt Judith (Mrs. Madan), whom Newton had kept informed of all that had taken place, they were pressed upon him.

Mrs. Madan before her marriage had the honour to be passionately admired by the poet Pope, who bestowed upon her the poetical name of Erinna. It was to her that Pope wrote the *Letters to a Lady*, published by Dodsley in 1769.

COWPER AND HIS HARES, PUSS AND TINEY.

After about fourteen months Cowper slowly regained his mental powers, and as he recovered he began to amuse himself with carpentering, drawing, gardening, and keeping pet animals. His three hares, Puss, Tiney, and Bess have obtained a world celebrity.

He also continued the delightful series of letters to his friends, William Unwin, Joseph Hill, and others.

A great change now took

* See the Author's "Life of William Cowper."

place in Cowper's mode of life; in 1780, the same year that Newton removed to London, he began to give himself up altogether to literary work.

Before leaving Olney, Newton introduced him to his friend, the Rev. William Bull of Newport Pagnell, who for so many years, was equally beloved by them both. Newton looked upon a quiet pipe with "Dear Taureau" as one of the chief pleasures of this life; and Cowper, though no smoker, who had even been satirical on smoking in one of his poems, seems never to have been so delighted as when he could get Bull and his pipe into the Summer-house---"the smoke-inhaling Bull," "always filling, never full."

OLNEY MARKET PLACE IN THE TIME OF COWPER.

We now come to the most interesting portion of Cowper's life---the period at Olney during which his principal works were produced. Hitherto he had written nothing of merit besides three or four hymns composed at St. Albans and Huntingdon, and sixty-six others at Olney; for his "Early Poems" are devoid of intrinsic value. His history as a poet really commences in 1780. In the course of that year, he wrote several short pieces for his own amusement; and then, at the instance of Mrs. Unwin, began and finished the "Progress of

Error." This was rapidly followed by "Truth," "Table-Talk," "Expostulation," "Hope," "Charity," "Conversation," and "Retirement." A few minor pieces were added; and the volume was published in March, 1782.

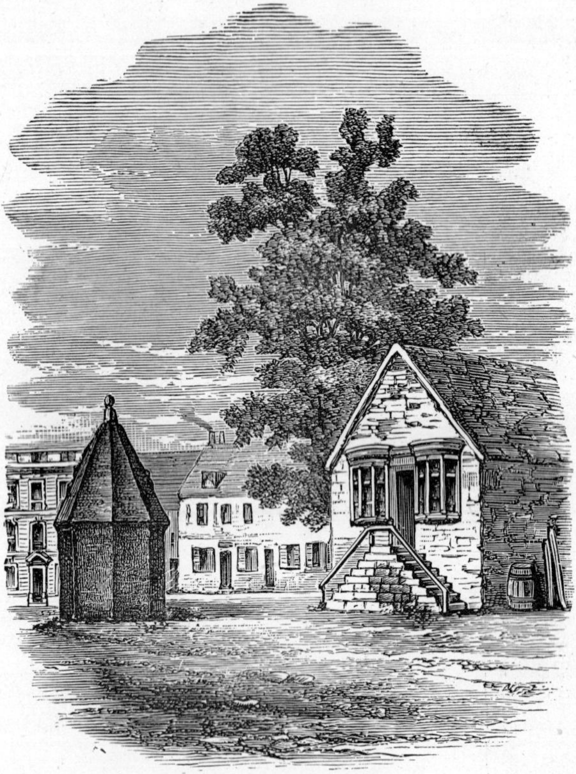

THE SHIEL HALL (TEEDON'S SCHOOL) AND ROUND HOUSE.

The ill-returns which Cowper had received from his kindness in educating and bringing up Dick Coleman did not deter a repetition of the experiment, and in 1781 we find him possessed of a second *protégée*, a little girl named Hannah

Willson, who was the daughter of Dick Coleman's wife by a former husband. Hannah had been received into Cowper's household solely from charitable motives, the idea being to train her for a useful servant. In his second *protégée* Cowper was no more fortunate than in his first, for Hannah Willson, though in a different way, proved as unworthy of the poet's kindness as Dick Coleman. Cowper's first reference to her is on July 22, 1781, when he describes to Newton a picnic in the spinnie. About this time too, or earlier, Cowper became acquainted with another person who was destined to exercise very great influence over his life—Samuel Teedon, a poor, egotistical and inordinately vain, but simple minded and fervently religious schoolmaster, who taught his scholars in the old building on the Market Place called the Shiel Hall.

LADY AUSTEN.

In the summer of 1781 Cowper became acquainted with Lady Austen; who was visiting at Clifton Reynes, and journeys to Clifton became very frequent. "John Gilpin" was published anonymously in November 1782, and in July 1783, at Lady Austen's suggestion, was commenced his great work, "The Task." *

CLIFTON CHURCH.

The acquaintance of the poet with Mr. John Courtenay Throckmorton (afterwards Sir John) commenced in May 1784. "You say well, my dear," he wrote to Lady Hesketh a few years later, "that in Mr. Throckmorton we have a peerless neighbour; we have so. In point of information on all subjects, in respect, too, of expression and address, and, in

* In 1888 was published "A Concordance to the Poetical Works of William Cowper," by John Neve.

short, everything that enters into the idea of a gentleman, I have not found his equal (not often) anywhere. Were I asked who in my judgment approaches nearest to him in all his amiable qualities and qualifications, I should certainly answer his brother George."

The path that Cowper usually took when visiting the Throckmorton grounds at Weston is the one that gradually rises from the close, called the Pightle, through several enclosures on the west side of Olney, and is parallel to the road leading from Olney to Weston, the highest portion being that called by Cowper in his letters "the Cliff," though it is not "a cliff, nor at all like one, but a beautiful terrace, sloping gently down to the Ouse." In the "Task," in which it is alluded to as "Yon eminence," Cowper describes the charming views commanded by it: the "slow winding Ouse," the square tower of Clifton church, the tall spire of Olney, "groves, heaths, and smoking villages remote."

From "the Cliff" he usually took his way to the Ho-brook, a diminutive stream that crosses the road midway between Olney and Weston. Bounded on one side by the Ho-brook is a long narrow plantation called, locally, the First Spinnie, but better known to readers of Cowper as the Shrubbery. It is threaded by a winding path, and in its midst stood the "Moss-house," a favourite haunt of Cowper's, which had on one side of it a weeping willow, and in front a beautiful circular sheet of water. It was an unpretentious stone structure, with thatched roof, covered with ivy and moss, and at a distance looked very like a great mushroom.

The following lines on the Shrubbery, which were written by Cowper in a time of affliction, were inserted in his first volume of poems:—

"Oh, happy shades—to me unblest!
  Friendly to peace, but not to me!
How ill the scene, that offers rest,
  And heart, that cannot rest, agree.

This glassy stream, that spreading pine,
  Those alders quiv'ring to the breeze,
Might soothe a soul less hurt than mine,
  And please, if anything could please.

The saint or moralist should tread
  This moss-grown alley musing, slow;
They seek, like me, the secret shade,
  But not, like me, to nourish woe.

Me, fruitful scenes, and prospects waste,
  Alike admonish not to roam;
These tell me of enjoyments past,
  And those of sorrows yet to come."

In the Moss-house was placed a board upon which were inscribed the poet's lines:—

"Here, free from riot's hated noise,
Be mine, ye calmer, purer joys,
  A book or friend bestows;
Far from the storms that shake the great
Contentment's gale shall fan my seat
  And sweeten my repose."

THE MOSS HOUSE.

But this board was stolen, so the poet put up another with the following lines, which are substantially the same as those in the sixth book of the "Task":—

"No noise is here, or none that hinders thought;
Stillness, accompanied with sounds like these,
Charms more than silence. Meditation here
May think down hours to moments. Here the heart
May give a useful lesson to the head,
And learning wiser grow without his books."

THE SECOND SPINNIE.

Keeping to the windings of the streamlet, and passing many a pleasant nook, we enter the field in front of the "Peasant's Nest"—no longer as formerly a picturesque thatch-roofed cottage, half hidden in foliage. Its trees have been felled, and the building itself is transformed into a prim-looking farmhouse. Still keeping to our streamlet or "weedy ditch," into which the peasant used to dip his bowl, we are brought to another plantation, the Second Spinnie, crowded with firs, pines, and yews, from which we emerge into the Chestnut Avenue :—

"Thanks to Benevolus, he spares me yet
These chestnuts ranged in corresponding rows,
And, though himself so polished, still reprieves
The obsolete prolixity of shade."

RUSTIC BRIDGE.

An abrupt descent leads to the "Rustic Bridge," and the "gulf" where "the willows" used to "dip their pendent boughs, stooping as if to drink." Ascending the steep walk that borders the northern extremity of the Park, we are brought to the Alcove, a small hexagonal structure, with three sides open, and quitting the Alcove, we presently find ourselves in the beautiful "Avenue of Lime Trees," of which Cowper writes :—

THE ALCOVE.

"How airy and how light the graceful arch,
Yet awful as the consecrated roof
Re-echoing pious anthems! while beneath
The checkered earth seems restless as a flood
Brush'd by the wind."

("Task," Book I.)

Cowper thus refers to the care that was taken to preserve its beauty (July 6, 1788) :—

THE AVENUE.

"By the help of the axe and the wood bill, which have of late been constantly employed in cutting out all straggling branches that intercepted the arch, Mr. Throckmorton has now defined it with such exactness that no cathedral in the world can show one of more magnificence or beauty. I bless myself that I live so near it; for, were it distant several miles, it would be well worth while to visit, merely as an object of taste; not to mention the refreshment of such a gloom both to the eyes and spirits."

URN IN WILDERNESS WITH EPITAPH TO FOP. SIR GEORGE AND LADY THROCKMORTON (CATHARINA).

The Wilderness, with its ceaseless caw of rooks, whither we are now walking, has still abundant charms; its walks, however, have not been "well-rolled" for many a day, and the monuments, adorned with bright green moss, and ivy, are in a dilapidated state. To some of the vanished glories of this spot, Cowper alludes in "Task," VI. Laburnum contributed its "streaming gold." There were lilacs, syringas, and Guelder roses. Hypericum presented her slender rods of flowers, mezereon her "blushing wreaths."

THE TEMPLE IN THE WILDERNESS.

(*As it appeared in the time of Cowper.*)

There was "Althæa with the purple eye," broom with blossoms, "Yellow and bright, as bullion unalloy'd," and luxuriant above all "The jasmine, throwing wide her elegant sweets."

The broad walk that borders the northern side of the Wilderness is ornamented with two monumental urns. Upon the pedestal of one is engraved the well-known epitaph, by Cowper, on Sir John Throckmorton's pointer :—

WESTON HALL. *(North Front.)*

"Here lies one who never drew
Blood himself, yet many slew;
Gave the gun its aim, and figure
Made in field, yet ne'er pulled trigger.
Armed men have gladly made
Him their guide, and him obeyed;
At his signified desire,
Would advance, present, and fire.
Stout he was, and large of limb,
Scores have fled at sight of him;
And to all this fame he rose,
By only following his nose.
Neptune was he called; not he
Who controls the boist'rous sea,
But of happier command
Neptune of the furrowed land:
And your wonder, vain, to shorten,
Pointer to Sir John Throckmorton."

On the pedestal of the other urn is an inscription written at the request of Mrs. Courtenay (Catharina), afterwards Lady Throckmorton, on a puppy named Fop.

EPITAPH ON FOP,

A DOG, BELONGING TO LADY THROCKMORTON.

Though once a puppy, and though Fop by name,
Here moulders one whose bones some honour claim;
No sycophant, although of spaniel race!
And though no hound, a martyr to the chase!
Ye squirrels, rabbits, leverets, rejoice!
Your haunts no longer echo to his voice.
This record of his fate exulting view,
He died worn out with vain pursuit of you!
"Yes!" the indignant shade of Fop replies,
"And worn with vain pursuit, man also dies!"

The most conspicuous object in the Wilderness, is the Gothic Temple, now sadly out of repair; and another interesting object, is the bust of Homer, on the pedestal of which is a Greek couplet from Cowper's pen, together with a translation by Hayley:—

"The sculptor? Nameless, though once dear to fame,
But this man bears an everlasting name."

Weston Hall, the ancient mansion of the Throckmortons, which stood on the left side of the road leading from Olney to Weston, just outside the village, was entirely demolished in 1827; and of its near appurtenances none are now standing except the iron gates with four stone piers, and a portion of the stabling and granary crowned by a cupola. It consisted of a quadrangle enclosing a court, and drawings are in existence of each of its fronts. The north, principal, or Queen Anne front, faced the park, and was built by Sir Robert Throckmorton about 1710. The rest of the exterior was partly in the Queen Anne style and partly Elizabethan, the most irregular portion being the west front, which had a porch, and was a perfect medley of chimneys, gabled projections, and windows, the last dotted about in the oddest manner imaginable.

Weston Hall, indeed, with the exception of its north front, was a most odd-looking place. Beautiful it certainly was not.

Nevertheless, with its pleasant prospects, its extensive library, its aviary and numerous other amenities, it was by no means wanting in attractions.

At the entrance of the village is still standing one of the gateways of the park; the other, which was similar in appearance, and stood on the side nearest Olney, has disappeared. The road in front of the house, which ran through the park (from which it was not railed off), was formerly a private one, and consequently the gates were shut at night. The public road ran between the hall and the river, but with the exception of the portion abutting upon the village street, where stands the socket of the ancient cross, has since been done away with.

The publication of "The Task" made its author famous, and his relations, who had previously had but little intercourse with him, were now only too pleased to communicate with him. Their letters were warmly welcomed; but the person with whom it gave him most pleasure to correspond was Lady Hesketh, and the series of letters to her is perhaps the most delightful in the language. As the reader is probably aware, the two most important editions of Cowper's letters are those of Grimshawe and Southey. The former, however, has the very serious blemish that in many of the letters it leaves out the very cream.

But even Southey's edition is extremely defective. In the first place, the so-called "Private Correspondence" having been refused him, he was unable to keep to chronological order; in the second, through his misfortune in being obliged to copy Hayley, many of his letters are mutilated, (though not so badly as those in Grimshawe); and in the third, many letters have been brought to light since. The author hopes before many months have passed, to be able to put into the hands of the public, the whole of Cowper's correspondence in consecutive order with annotations.

In June, 1786, Lady Hesketh visited Olney, and stayed at the Vicarage till the following November; then, thinking that a change of residence would be beneficial to Cowper, she hired for him the house called Weston Lodge, to which he removed on the 15th.

V.

WESTON UNDERWOOD.

Weston Lodge, a large and comfortable house in the middle of the village, was the residence of Cowper, from November, 1786, to July 1795. In a letter to Mrs. Hill (November 5, 1793) he speaks of some of the advantages of his situation:—

"The opposite object," to the Lodge, "and the only one, is an orchard, so well planted, and with trees of such growth, that we seem to look into a wood, or rather to be surrounded by one. Thus, placed as we are in the midst of a village, we have none of those disagreeables that belong to such a position, and the village itself is one of the prettiest I know; terminated at one end by the church tower, seen through the trees, and at the other by a very handsome gateway, opening into a fine grove of elms, belonging to our neighbour Courtenay." The front of the house was ornamented with vines and jessamines. The shrubbery, which a later owner converted into an orchard, was "very generally admired, being a delightful little labyrinth, composed of flowering shrubs, and adorned with gravel walks, having convenient seats placed at appropriate distances." Of the "lonely winding walk" in this shrubbery, Cowper speaks in his fragment "The Four Ages," and he gives the following amusing account of the erection of an arbour in it:—

"I said to Sam—'Sam, build me a shed in the garden with anything you can find, and make it rude and rough like one of those at Eartham.'—'Yes, sir,' says Sam, and straightway laying his own noddle and the carpenter's noddle together, has built me a thing fit for Stow Gardens. Is not this vexatious? I threaten to inscribe it thus:—

'Beware of building! I intended
Rough logs and thatch, and thus it ended.'

But my Mary says, I shall break Sam's heart, and the carpenter's too, and will not consent to it."

In this shrubbery stood the bust of Homer (now in the Wilderness) presented to Cowper by his nephew, John Johnson, which drew from the former the sonnet thus commencing:—

"Kinsman beloved, and as a son, by me!
When I behold the fruit of thy regard,
The sculptured form of my old favourite bard,
I reverence feel for him, and love for thee."

SUN-DIAL.

Another present of Johnson's to Cowper, was a "smart sun-dial, mounted on a smart stone pedestal." (See Letter of 4th of Sept., 1793.)

This sun-dial, after Cowper left Weston, was removed by the Throckmortons to the Hall Garden, and in 1828, it was placed where it now stands, in the garden of the priest's house, and on or near the site of the porch that belonged to the west front of the mansion. The only inscription on it is:—

"Walter Gough, No. 21 Middle Row, Holborn, London."

In November 1784, a few days after the completion of the "Tirocinium," Cowper had commenced a translation of Homer, and he devoted almost the whole of his time to it. Within a fortnight after his arrival at Weston, a heavy calamity fell upon him and Mrs. Unwin. This was the death of her only son, the Rev. William Unwin, of Stock. Cowper was now fifty-five.

The shock of his friend's death proved too severe for him, and in January 1787, he was deranged for the fourth time. In about six months, however, he had suddenly recovered, and resumed at once his Homeric labours.

THE DOG AND THE WATER-LILY.

About this time, occurred the feat of Cowper's dog Beau, which is immortalised in the well-known poem of "The Dog and the Water Lily." It is thus referred to in the letter of June 27, 1788: "Walking by the river side, I observed some water-lilies floating at a little distance from the bank. I had a desire to gather one, and, having your long cane in my hand, by the help of it, endeavoured to bring one of them within my reach. But the attempt proved vain, and I walked forward. Beau had all the while observed me very attentively. Returning soon after toward the same place, I observed him plunge into the river, while I was about forty yards distant from him; and, when I had nearly reached the spot, he swam to land with a lily in his mouth, which he came and laid at my foot." The incident occurred near Goosey Bridge, close to Olney.

The Dog Beau (stuffed)
in the possession of the Rev.d D.r Johnson

The taxidermist has supplied the lily with convolvulus leaves!

On February 25, 1790, Cowper received from his niece, Mrs. Bodham, "the only picture of his mother to be found in all the world," a picture which he prized "more highly than the richest jewel in the British crown," and which inspired the beautiful elegy already alluded to and quoted. In May 1791, he commenced a poem on "The Four Ages—Infancy, Youth, Manhood, and Old Age," hoping to produce a work of about the same length as "The Task." But of this intended poem, only thirty-eight lines were written; it was laid aside for the lines on Yardley Oak, and this second remarkable fragment was in its turn laid aside for his notes on Milton. This brings us again to the subject of Samuel Teedon.

COWPER'S SHADOW.

Whilst Cowper lived at Olney, he had regarded Teedon as a good Christian, but at the same time as a vain and somewhat obtrusive man. But as years wept on, things changed, and at length, Cowper came to believe, that Teedon was especially favoured by Providence, in consequence of which, by degrees, extraordinary to say, the refined and gifted poet got to regard the vain and eccentric schoolmaster, as a kind of Delphic oracle. Cowper had seen visions, and dreamed dreams, and heard voices. Teedon in like manner received, as he took them to be, revelations from God. But there was this difference: Cowper believed himself a man whom God abhorred; Teedon regarded himself as heaven's special favourite. Consequently, whenever in doubt, Cowper had recourse to Teedon.

That Teedon was sincere in his convictions we have no reason to doubt. He endeavoured to use his influence for the poet's good, urging him to keep himself continually occupied, encouraging him to be frequent in prayer, and assuring him, that God in His own time would remove the terrible burden of his life. Moreover, though to interpret them at all was presumptuous, he always put on Cowper's dreams the brightest possible interpretations.

COWPER'S OAK.

When the question arose, whether the editorship of Milton, should be undertaken it was Teedon that Cowper consulted, and Teedon, after much prayer, obtained from Heaven, that it was certainly expedient that the poet should engage in the work. Consequently, Milton was gone forward with, but it proved a complete failure, and Cowper often wished "this Miltonic trap" had never caught him; but out of it, grew his acquaintance with the amiable Hayley, who afterwards became his biographer. In December 1791, Mrs. Unwin was seized with paralysis, and although she soon recovered, was never actually herself again. May 1792 saw Hayley at Weston; and in August of the same year Cowper and Mrs. Unwin paid the return visit to Eartham, near Chichester, where they remained for six weeks.

Whilst at Hayley's house at Eartham Cowper's portrait was drawn by Romney. A few weeks previous it had been painted by Abbot. A year later it was drawn by Lawrence.

There exist altogether seven different likenesses of the poet.

1. A miniature of Cowper, as a lad, in the posession of Sir Charles Dilke.

2. A newly discovered pastel, by John Russell, R.A., "The Prince of Crayon Portrait Painters." Russell was born in 1745, when Cowper was fourteen years old. The very youthful appearance of the poet suggests that the picture was done before 1763, when he quitted the Temple. The poet at this time, was about thirty-two, and the artist only 18.

3. A shadow or profile taken at Olney.

4. An oil painting by Abbot. Painted in July 1792 at Weston.

5. A portrait in crayons by Romney. Drawn in August and September 1792 at Eartham.

6. A sketch by (Sir) Thomas Lawrence. Drawn at Weston in October 1793.

7. A painting now in the possession of Earl Cowper, at Penshangar, Herts. It was painted after the poet's death, probably from the portraits of Abbot and Lawrence, and is ascribed to Jackson, R.A.

Abbot's oil painting represents the poet in a periwig, green coat, yellow waistcoat, and breeches. The desk represented is the one already spoken of as the gift of his cousin Thedora. Writing to Hayley, (July 15, 1792), Cowper says:—

> "Abbot is painting me so true,
> That (trust me) you would stare,
> And hardly know, at the first view,
> If I were here or there."

Romney's portrait was a "masterly and faithful resemblance," but it had an "air of wildness in it expressive of a disordered mind, which the shock produced by the paralytic attack of

Mrs. Unwin, was rapidly impressing on his countenance."

In Lawrence's portrait, as in Romney's, the poet is represented in the cap which he was accustomed to wear in a morning, presented to him by Lady Hesketh—the same immortalised in his lines entitled "Gratitude:"—

> "This cap, that so stately appears,
> With ribbon-bound tassel on high,
> Which seems by the crest that it rears
> Ambitious of brushing the sky;
> This cap to my cousin I owe,
> She gave it, and gave me beside,
> Wreathed into an elegant bow,
> The ribbon with which it is tied."

COWPER BY LAWRENCE.

Drawn at Weston in October 1793.

After their return to Weston in September, Mrs. Unwin's health rapidly declined, and she at length sank into a state of second childishness. The worse she became, however, the brighter burned Cowper's affection for her; and it was in the autumn of 1793, whilst she was in this pitiable state, that he wrote those affecting stanzas "To Mary" of which the following are three of the most beautiful:—

"Thy spirits have a fainter flow,
I see thee daily weaker grow;
'Twas my distress that brought thee low,
My Mary!

Thy needles, once a shining store,
For my sake restless heretofore,
Now rust disused, and shine no more,
My Mary!

Thy silver locks, once auburn bright,
Are still more lovely in my sight,
Than golden beams of orient light,
My Mary!"

THE LODGE, WESTON UNDERWOOD.

The beautiful sonnet commencing, "Mary! I want a lyre with other strings," was written in the preceeding May.

The anxiety occasioned to Cowper by Mrs. Unwin's illness now began to tell upon him; his gloom and melancholy came on again, and once more he sank into a state bordering on imbecility, from which he never fully recovered. A change of scene was now thought to be desirable, and accordingly his affectionate kinsman Johnson decided to convey the invalids into Norfolk.

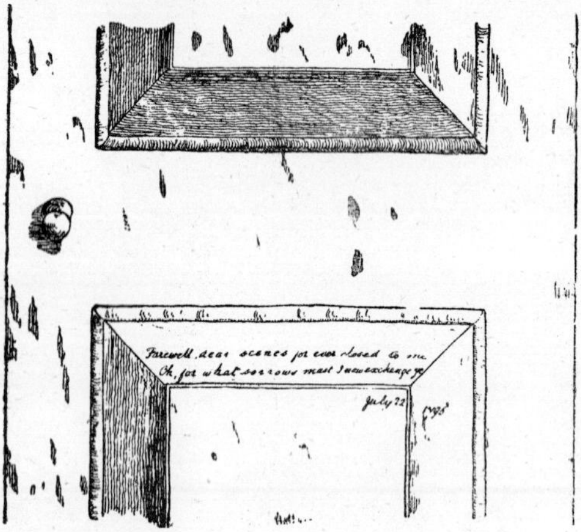

THE SHUTTER.

When Cowper left Weston for Norfolk neither he nor his friends intended anything further than a temporary absence: but still he had a presentiment that he should never return, and it was with this feeling in his mind that he wrote the oft-quoted lines on the panel of the window-shutter in his bedroom:—

> "Farewell, dear scenes, for ever closed to me;
> Oh, for what sorrows must I now exchange ye!"

Below them are two dates written thus:—

July 22
——28, 1795.

The second date is accounted for by the circumstance that

the removal from Weston took place, not on the day expected, but nearly a week after.

Under these were originally four more lines, which ran as follows:—

> "Me miserable! how could I escape
> Infinite wrath and infinite despair!
> Whom Death, Earth, Heaven, and Hell consigned to ruin,
> Whose friend was God, but God swore not to aid me!
> July 27, '95."

VI.

NORFOLK, 1795-1800.

They first proceeded to the village of North Tuddenham, near East Dereham, where they were accommodated with an untenanted parsonage house, in which they were received by Mr. Johnson's sister and her friend Miss Perowne. In August the invalids were taken to the village of Mundesley, on the Norfolk coast, so as to have the benefit of the sea air, and here they resided until October. When Dr. Johnson and his invalids had explored all the walks in the neighbourhood of Mundesley, they made a journey by way of Cromer, Holt, and Fakenham to look at Dunham Lodge, a house to which they removed in October.

The few years spent in Norfolk were sad in the extreme.

In the summer of 1796, the invalids were at Mundesley again, and finally, in October of that year, they removed to East Dereham.

Mrs. Unwin died on December 17, 1796, at the age of seventy-two. Cowper never afterwards mentioned her name.

On December 20, 1799, he wrote his last original piece, those pathetic and despondent lines entitled "The Castaway," and he died on the 25th of April 1800, in the sixty-ninth year of his age. He was buried on the 2d of May, in St. Edmund's Chapel, in the church of East Dereham, where a monument was erected to his memory, with an inscription from the pen of Hayley.

Thus with all its troubles and all its fears, passed away the spirit of the gentle Cowper.

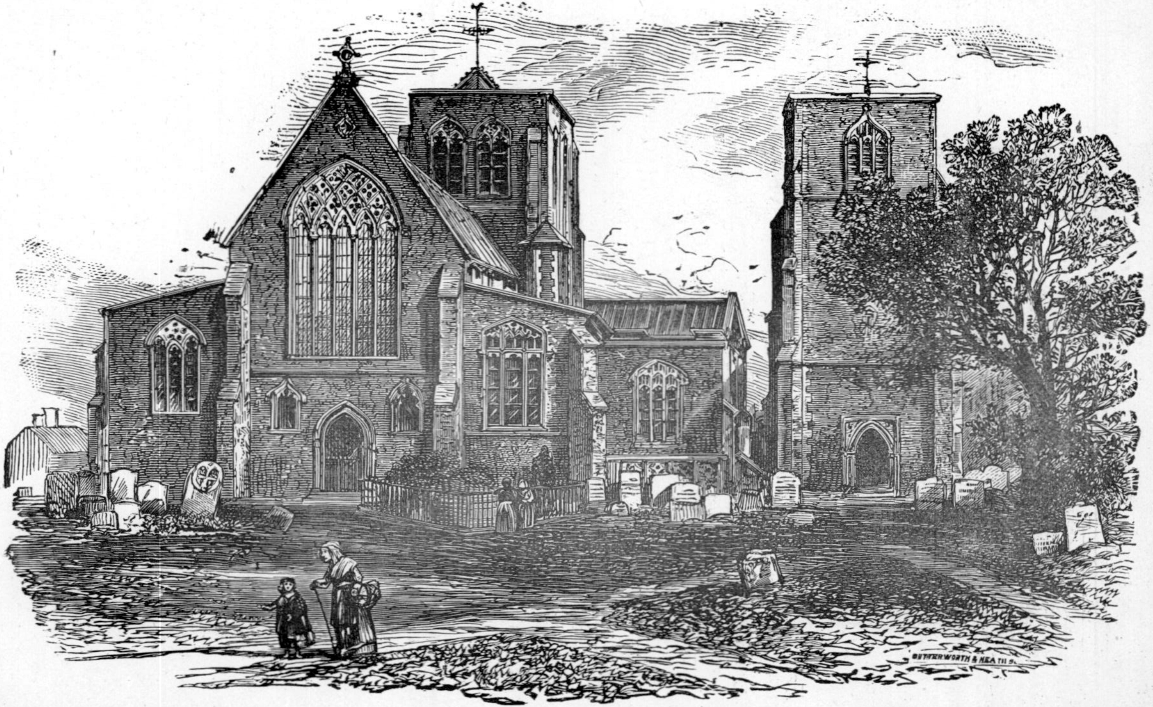

EAST DEREHAM CHURCH. *(Norfolk).*

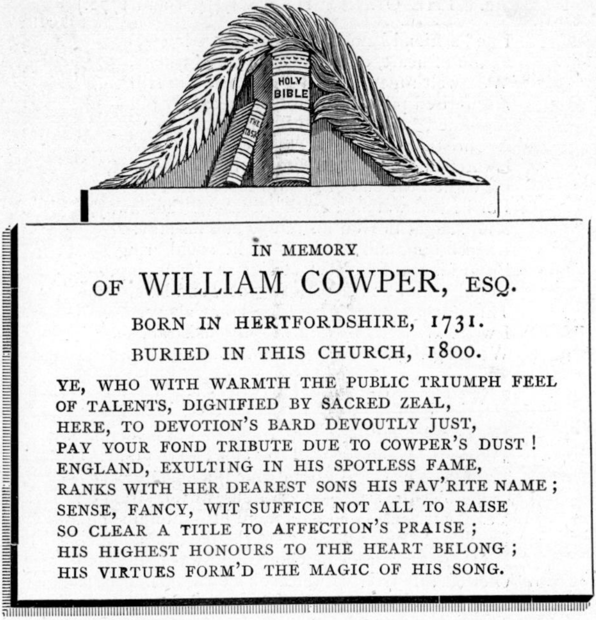

COWPER'S MONUMENT, IN EAST DEREHAM CHURCH, NORFOLK.

LINES ON COWPER.

*By the Rev. John Newton.**

I. FRIENDSHIP (Oct. 1767-Jan. 1773).

Strangers we were, and sojourners; our home
A world to sin, and death, and sorrow known:
Yet known to *hope*,—for there the Son of God
Had left His blessing when that world he trod:
Blessings unnumbered had his hand bestowed,
And one was—friendship on the pilgrim's road.

---

* These beautiful lines have never before appeared in print except in an obscure little collection of twenty-five of Newton's letters, issued from Edinburgh in 1842.

2. THE OLNEY HYMNS (1771 and 1772.)

I had a friend beloved; and well we knew
Union of heart, confiding, fond, and true.
We dwelt together, and I watched him still
An untired pilgrim toward the heavenly hill—
A soldier, 'mid a troop of hostile foes,—
A Christian, finding 'neath the cross repose.
I watched him, and admired, when lowly bent,
He owned the cup of grief in mercy sent;
For he had watched earth's treasures fade away,
And sought in God his refuge and his stay.
I heard him, and admired, for he could bring
From his soft harp such strains as angels sing,—
Could tell of free salvation, grace, and love,
Till angels listened from their home above.
I woke my lyre to join his rapturous strain—
We sang together of the Lamb once slain.

3. COWPER IN THE DEPTHS. (Jan. 1773-May 1774.)

Thus passed our life away. The sun had shone
Till years (as mortals call them) six were gone;
Then (as Eternal Wisdom willed) a change
Came o'er the scene—mysterious, awful, strange!
Yes, he was changed! no more his grateful song
Proclaimed him happier than the day was long;
No more his music-wakening hand was flung
O'er earthly lyre, with heaven's own amaranths hung.
How shall I tell the tale? he knows not here
The sigh of anguish, nor the pang of fear;
No longer dwells in frame of clay confined
That emanation from the eternal mind.

4. NEWTON WATCHES OVER HIM.

My friend I watched thee, when that earthly frame
Encircled (union strange) the ethereal flame,
And there were hidden sufferings, that no eye
Of skilled and kind physician* could descry;
And there were doubts, and fears, and terrors given,
Till peace on earth was gone, and hope of heaven.

5. AND ENDEAVOURS TO COMFORT HIM.

My friend, I watched thee treading day by day
Through the dim valley of death's shadowy way.
Did I not walk with thee? Did I not turn
From brighter scenes, these mysteries to learn,
When thou didst mourn the loss of heavenly grace,

* Dr. Cotton, Cowper's St. Albans physician, to whom Newton applied.

And deem that God had turned away his face !
That could not be ; His oath was firmly taken—
"My people shall not, cannot be forsaken ;
Their earthly sorrows make them doubt my love,
They will not doubt it in my heaven above."

THE SUPPOSED MEETING OF COWPER AND NEWTON IN HEAVEN.

My friend, my friend ! and have we met again,
Far from the home of woe, the home of men ;
And hast thou taken thy glad harp once more,
Twined with far lovelier wreaths than e'er before ;
And is thy strain more joyous and more loud,
While circle round thee heaven's attentive crowd ?

Oh ! let thy memory wake ! I told thee so ;
I told thee thus would end thy heaviest woe ;
I told thee that thy God would bring thee here,
And God's own hand would wipe away thy tear
While I should claim a mansion by thy side,
I told thee so—for our Emmanuel died.

APPENDIX.

The Rev. John Newton, Cowper's friend, died in his eighty-third year, on Dec. 21, 1807, and was buried at St. Mary Woolnoth's, London. In January, 1883, his remains, and those of his wife, were removed to Olney churchyard, where a handsome monument to their memory has recently been erected.

The Rev. Christopher Stephenson was vicar of Olney from 1800 to 1815. His grandson, the Rev. J. H. Stephenson, is Rector of Lympsham, near Weston-Super-Mare, and Prebendary of Wells.

The distinguished Evangelical preacher, the Rev. Henry Gauntlett, resided at Olney, from 1811 till his death in 1834.

Dr. Henry John Gauntlett, the great Church musician, was his eldest son. Dr. Gauntlett died in 1876.

A grandson of Dr. Gauntlett, Master William Alfred Basil Deane Gauntlett, who made his début on Thursday, Nov. 30th., 1893, at the Scotch concert, in the Royal Albert Hall, inherits his grandfather's gifts. The little fellow, who is even now only in his ninth year, was born at Kensington, in January 1885. By the time he was four, he could play the scales perfectly. When only five he played the overture and incidental music at some private theatricals. Until till two years ago, he studied with his aunt, Miss Mildred Gauntlett ; then he was placed under the guidance of Signor Carlo Ducci, and now he is going through a course of study under Mr. William Carter. The career of this youthful genius will be watched with intense interest.

COWPER SCHOOL,

OLNEY, BUCKS.

PRINCIPALS:

Mr. THOMAS WRIGHT,

Author of "The Life of William Cowper," etc.,

AND

Mrs. THOMAS WRIGHT,

Works of

THOMAS WRIGHT,

Principal of Cowper School, Olney.

The Life of William Cowper.

Large Demy 8vo 742 pages, 21 illustrations, 21/- Edition de Luxe 30/-

LONDON: FISHER UNWIN.

The standard biography of Cowper—*Daily News.* Mr. Wright's Cowper puts all former lives of the poet in the shade—*Saturday Review.* Mr. Wright has pursued a new method in reading Cowper's correspondence in consecutive order, and claims thereby to have discovered " what may be described as the central incident of the poet's life. This incident was a dream—*The Times.* One of the most ambitious work of the kind—*Scotsman.* Deeply interesting—*Daily Telegraph.* A book of unflagging interest—*Literary World.* Mr. Wright has given us a better picture of Cowper at home than has been drawn by any other biographer—*Standard.*

The Life of Daniel Defoe.

In the press.

Large Demy 8vo about 800 pages, 21/- Edition de Luxe, 30/- 25 illustrations, including recently discovered portraits of Defoe and his friends. This work contains a great quantity of entirely new facts concerning the eminent novelist, and throws much fresh light on his private life. When Mr. Wright was in the midst of this work, Mr. George Saintsbury, the eminent critic, wrote as follows:—" I am very glad to hear that you are at work on Defoe. All the present lives are inadequate. His works too are in a shocking condition, unidentified to a great extent, and utterly unedited almost everywhere. Your " Cowper" which I read with a great deal of pleasure last week, makes me look forward to any attempt of yours on the subject.

The Life of Charles Dickens.

Preparing for publication.

Large Demy 8vo 750 pages, 21/- Edition de Luxe, 30/- 20 Illustrations. A great mass of entirely new material concerning Dickens, including unpublished letters, has been placed in Mr. Wright's hands for embodiment in this work. At present, the only life of Dickens of any consequence is the lamentably imperfect biography by Forster, which some wag pertinently styled: " The Life of John Forster with Incidental Reminiscences of Charles Dickens."

" It is gratifying to hear that much concerning Charles Dickens of which Forster was ignorant is to be told to his admirers, under your auspices; and your laudable enterprise cannot fail to evoke sympathy and to achieve success."—*Dean Hole.*

The Town of Cowper,

Or the Literary and Historical Associations of Olney and its Neighbourhood (2nd Edition), 16 illustrations, Cr. 8vo, 3/6. LONDON: S. LOW & CO.

A delightful volume—*Leisure Hour.* A model volume—*Pall Mall Gazette.* Mr. Wright's pleasant *mèlange* of antiquities and history—*Saturday Review.* A delightful volume—*Daily News.* A pleasantly written volume—*Illustrated London News.* All lovers of the gentle, unobtrusive Cowper will hail this volume with delight.

The Loved Haunts of Cowper.

Cr. 8vo, 2/- With 40 illustrations.

This work is an abbreviation of Mr. Wright's large work, "The Life of William Cowper." It contains the poem by Newton, entitled, "The supposed meeting of Cowper and Newton in Heaven."

Turvey and Legh Richmond.

(2nd Edition). By the Rev. G. F. W. Munby, M.A., and Thos. Wright.

Cr. 8vo, 2/- LONDON: F. KIRBY.

Should be read by all who are familiar with "The Annals of the Poor."—*The News*.

Olney and Dr. Carey, or Serampore Letters,

Being the unpublished letters of Dr. Carey the eminent missionary. With an introduction by Thomas Wright. Cr. 8vo, 9 photographs, chiefly views of Olney, 6/-. LONDON & NEW YORK: PUTNAMS.

The introduction is by Mr. Wright, the learned author of the latest life of the poet Cowper. Mr. Wright's name is sufficient guarantee that the work is done thoroughly, with a real literary finish—*Reigate Chronicle.*

The Mystery of St. Dunstan's.

(2nd Edition). 5/- LONDON: S. LOW & CO.

Defoe is introduced as one of the characters in a very natural and skilful way—*The Guardian*. Mr. Wright, the accomplished historian of Olney, comes before us with a realistic and sensational story of Fleet Street in 1724, which fully justifies its title. "The Mystery of St. Dunstan's "is an excellent and engrossing tale, full of exciting incidents leading up to an unexpected *dénoûment—Athenæum*. One of the best kept secrets in recent fiction—*Daily Chronicle.*

The Chalice of Carden.

Mr. Wright's Bedfordshire and Buckinghamshire story, 3 illustrations, 6/- LONDON: SKEFFINTON & SON.

A faithful study of Buckinghamshire and its ways in the time of the '45, set forth in admirable and attractive style, as we have a right to expect from the learned and accomplished author of "The Town of Cowper—*Athenæum.* As amusing as Pickwick. Mr. Wright has written a very clever story—*Literary Churchman.*

The Blue Firedrake.

(3rd Edition.) Mr. Wright's Northamptonshire story of the last witch burnt in England. 10 illustrations. 3/6. LONDON: SIMPKIN & MARSHALL.

A weird and thrilling tale of which the plot is well constructed, and, the interest never for a moment flags—*Beds Standard.* Gruesomely fascinating—*Pall Mall Gazette.* The story is an exciting one—in parts, creepy—*Northampton Herald.*

95